ADVENTURES IN PSYCHODRAMA

Dr. Peter A Olsson

www.drpeterolsson.com

ISBN: 197403738X
ISBN 13: 9781974037384

ADVENTURES IN PSYCHODRAMA THERAPY
INTRODUCTION

During my training in psychiatry I was fortunate to have been taught about psychodrama. Jorge Valles MD used psychodrama to treat alcoholic patients at the Houston VA Hospital. Valles patiently taught me psychodrama and was my psychodrama mentor. I have found psychodrama group therapy to be very helpful in treating addictions, marital, vocational, family, and psychosomatic problems. Basic techniques of psychodrama like role-playing, role reversal, doubling, the soliloquy, empty chair, the narrator and magic shop can be helpful in group or individual therapy...even medical teaching.

Classic Psychodrama involves a **stage area** (Preferably elevated), the **director, protagonist(s), antagonists, the audience, alter-egos** and **doubles**. Hospital staff and other patients are asked to assume roles in the patient situation on focus. Efforts are made to dramatize the actual emotional experience and conflicts in the patient's life situation. Such participation is essential to the therapeutic group process. The audience group is a vital part of the therapeutic group process. Unlike the Hollywood movie director who stays at a distance back of the camera it is crucial that the director stay close to the patient who has chosen to have his life situation on focus. In classic psychodrama, the director like the captain of a ship or airplane is in charge. Staff and other patients may occasionally make suggestions but the final clinical decision rests with the director. The director needs to stay in tune with the protagonist's facial expression, tension, emotions as he or she sets the scenes and implements various psycho-drama techniques. The psychodrama techniques like **the soliloquy**, **the empty chair** (Where an important person in the patient's life is imagined to be sitting and be confronted), **doubling** of the patient's likely inner unconscious or preconscious thoughts, **role-reversal** with an antagonist and focus on a patient's dream or fantasy can be very powerful therapeutically...But, for a fragile, highly anxious or bor-derline psychotic patient care must be taken with dosing of conflicts confronted in the patient.

More Detail about the Three Basic Psychodrama Techniques

1. Role Reversal---At the initiative of the director, the patient is asked to suddenly switch roles with the person to whom he is talking. For example, a husband embroiled with his wife in a heated conflict situation is abruptly instructed to take her role in the scene. This technique can jolt the patient with sud-den stunning insight.
2. Doubling---The director asks a staff member or other patient in the group to stand close to or behind the patient and speak out clearly what the inner thoughts, feelings or perceptions of the patient apparently are. These thoughts are pretended not to be heard unless the patient choses to voice them. Doubling is often crucial at the time a role reversal is implemented by the director.
3. Soliloquy---The scene is halted by the director and a key per-son in the scene usually the patient on focus is urged to de-liver a lengthy monologue about his feelings, doubts, fears, insights or contemplated plans of action. A double can assist the patient with this process.

Classic psychodrama has **five phases**. Warm-up, Setting-the-scene, Rising action, Climax, Declining action /Resolution and Share-back.

An actual stage or regularly designated stage area, stage furniture and props (If possible), are important to enliven the therapeutic process. At all times during the psychodrama the director needs to stay close to the patient protagonist. The director must set the scene(s) as accurately as possible, and always try to see the psychodrama stage-world as the patient is experiencing it. A scene may be shifted fluidly between past, present or future by the director. Past, present and future may even be represented simultaneously on the psychodrama therapy stage. A scene may be repeated several times (therapeutic instant- replays), in search of conflict resolution. Resolution and mastery of a conflict and changed behavior in actual action (not merely words) is celebrated and applauded.

After the therapeutic action, the audience group participates in a **"share-back"** group process. The patient who shared his or her life scenes with the group sits on stage next to the director. The audience must best not analyze and interpret the patient protagonist's experience that has been enacted. Audience members and the patient on focus both benefit from shared experiences. New and helpful approaches to conflict situations may occur to anyone attending the psychodrama therapy session. Such sharing is the heart of the share-back phase. Discussions by patient's other than the patient on focus during that psychodrama occasion is crucial. The audience share-back conclusion of classic psychodrama highlights how psychodrama therapy is a true form of group therapy. The action scenes in a psychodrama session bring behavioral change, conflict resolution by tangible action, and catharsis of emotion. Not merely passive intellectual discussion.

One basic truth in psychiatry and psychodynamic psychotherapy is that a significant portion of the human mind is outside of conscious awareness and the unconscious mind contains irrational elements. (Very often people don't make sense or act sensibly.)

Freud discovered that when a therapist tries to get involved with a troubled or not even very troubled human being, TRANSFERENCE occurs. The person/patient transfers on to the therapist images and feelings that reflect early childhood relationships with parents, siblings and parental surrogates. These projections onto the therapist contain love and tender feelings, as well as hate, fear, rage, even murderous elements. At times in particularly fragile persons who have suffered early loss, trauma, cruelty---especially early remorseless brutality---the hate and rage can erupt and be directed at even the kindest therapist. Now, let's enter some actual dramatic adventures in psychodrama therapy.

1

ASSAULT ON A THERAPIST DURING A HOSPITAL PSYCHODRAMA

Jack at the urging of his small group, volunteered to work on his addiction problem in our inpatient psychodrama. Jack had been treated coldly and cruelly by his father. The director of the psychodrama session called on me to role play Jack's cruel father. Jack had lost one arm via an infection that had resulted from a beating at the hands of his father. The patient had one of those metal arm-hand prostheses with metal graspers. As the psychodrama scene unfolded and I played the verbally cruel father to the hilt. Jack t suddenly swung his metal arm at me. I saw it coming out of the corner of my eye as it glinted in sunlight coming from the day hospital window nearby. I ducked. Jack's metal hand and arm embedded in the sheet rock wall. An aid and I held Jack down and he began to sob.

Jacks small group members in the large psychodrama group audience described to him what had happened. Jack said the last thing he remembered was his father's sneering cruel face and words.

The patient begged my forgiveness but more important was the dramatic way he began to see how his severe alcohol problem was covering over his unresolved murderous rage at his father. As he worked on that issue over the ensuing months, he stayed sober and became much less depressed. I saw him in a follow-up meeting a year later. He had been sober for that year and was working regularly. He hugged me and said---"Thanks Dad, now I have some real friends, not just drinking buddies."

I might have been hurt or even killed. Transference and its resolution blazed in that psychodrama And resolution of Jack's inner rage at his father/himself began that day at psychodrama.

I once took custody of a machete that one of my patients was fearful he would use on me and our treatment team group. Not all clinics have a security guard or a metal detector. They obviously should. If psychodrama therapy like all therapy is done effectively, powerful emotions are stirred. Often such drama and catharsis is necessary for a cure to begin.

2

ELEPHANT LADY (A SHORT STORY)

The following short story depicts the inner life of a woman I/we worked with in psychodrama.

My name is Ellen. I love elephants. I am fifty years old, but I look sixty-five. My legs are the size of elephant legs. The only fat, wrinkled, thick-legged old lady that anyone ever loved was Eleanor Roosevelt. They overlooked her body, and loved her mind and spirit. I have a mediocre mind and no spirit left. In fact, my mind feels like Chubby Checker doing the "Twist" in a swimming pool filled with molasses. My sense of humor disappeared six months ago, and my attitude makes accounts of menopause sound like Madonna's sex life.

Speaking of sex life, that old wino downstairs doesn't even stop by with his elegant bottle of Thunderbird on Friday nights anymore. I can't get a good night's sleep with or without alcohol. I read an article in *O: The Oprah Magazine,* and it said that depressed people lose their appetite. I cannot stop eating, even after my feet disappeared out of sight beyond the belly fat that forms a wide, quivering, natural apron around my former waistline.

My daughter Lucy loves me, but she doesn't know me. She seldom can stand to be around me for more than twenty minutes. In America, few young people find an old person interesting. Lin Chang, my now dead and former neighbor, said that old people are respected in China. My daughter never even introduced herself to Lin Chang. Lucy loves me but she doesn't listen to me. I want to move to China. Lucy is a dumb bitch!

You say, "How can I say that about my own daughter?" My first clue was, when it dawned on me that she didn't have the vaguest idea about how important my elephants are to me. Elephants are beautiful, powerful, intelligent, and graceful. They are not clumsy and awkward. I love my elephants. They surround me and protect me. I have over one hundred elephants, and I love every one of them. They never forget me.

Anyway, my daughter did convince me to get free medical care at the VA Hospital for my headaches. Those five years I spent in the navy after high school might be good for something after all. In the VA hospital system, they call it "service connection." I got so many headaches when I was in the navy. The navy doctors never could figure out what caused them. I got a medical discharge from the navy with 10 percent "service connection." In other words, the US Navy caused 10 percent of my headaches in life.

Every time my daughter comes to visit me, I get a terrible headache. Every time I get a job and the boss makes unreasonable demands on me, I get a terrible headache. Thunderbird wine gives me a headache, but my elephants take my headache away within an hour. They comfort me in every room of my apartment.

The VA general doctors couldn't find out a physical cause for my headaches and wanted me to see a psychiatrist. It was free, so I went to the appointment. Dr. Nelson wasn't like those psychiatrists you see in movies or on TV. He didn't have a beard. He is young, good looking and he listened to me for almost a whole hour! I mean, he really listened! Have you ever had anyone listen to you with complete attention for a whole hour? It felt eerie. I liked his blue eyes and they looked straight at me. He listened to the names of all my elephants and didn't joke about whether I was a Republican or not. I showed him my smallest elephant and a picture of my largest one. I could tell that he cared about me, but I really cannot tell you exactly why.

Dr. Nelson asked just a few questions and they were mainly about Lucy and me. Nelson thought I could get help with my headaches at the VA Day Hospital program. He said it would be tough for me at first, but he thought I had the guts to stick with it until I got better. He said that the Day Hospital uses individual therapy, group therapy, and psychodrama to help people put their problems into words. Then people could figure out their own answers. The more I could put my feelings, anger, and fears into words, Nelson told me, the less I would have to keep tension stored up in my neck and scalp muscles. So, I agreed to try the Day Hospital for three months. What the hell, it was free.

The VA Hospital is huge, but off near the back gate is a small building with its own little parking lot. When I drove up at least I could park. I was early enough so that the white-lined parking spaces were not so filled up that I had to enter one space between two already parked cars. Phew!

The Day Hospital receptionist was kind, supportive, and helpful with all the paperwork. Computers are supposed to decrease paperwork, but they just generate it faster. In the Day Hospital there are groups A, B, and C. I was put in therapy group B and it was a "Lulu." There were nineteen members, twenty including me. Five were bald or balding World War II or Korean War vets and six were longhaired Vietnam vets, some of whom were still fighting "post-war rejection syndrome."

I told the young "Nam whiners," as I called them, that they should try being a woman abandoned after one year of marriage with a one-year-old baby by a big brave marine! I didn't say my piece until the very end of group, so there were a few shocked stares. I got a couple of warm smiles but I never even got to trust anyone enough to mention my elephants. I did talk a little bit about Lucy during the next two group meetings.

PSYCHODRAMA DAY AND ME BY ELLEN

Thursday was psychodrama day at the Day Hospital. Groups A, B, and C were all at the psychodrama together. That made thirty-six patients and about ten staff and students in the audience. The psychodrama director was a tall, overweight psychiatrist with a warm smile and a relaxed style. His name was Simon Solomon. He sat in a chair up on a slightly elevated stage and chatted with some of the patients he worked with at previous psychodramas. Some of the guys talked about progress they made because of work at previous psychodramas. Other patients spoke about ongoing, unresolved problems. Solomon urged them to work further on them in psychodrama or in their small group therapy sessions. I began to get a headache.

Solomon asked the group, "Does anyone have a situation to work on today at psychodrama?"

There was a silence and Solomon must have noticed my frown and self-messaging of my forehead. He looked at me sympathetically and asked, "Are you okay? You look worried. By the way, what's your name?"

"My name is Ellen," I said. "I have a headache, but don't want psychodrama." I hoped my frown would send him in search of another victim.

Solomon softly said, "Ellen, we find that headaches, stomachaches, backaches, and other body symptoms can be worked with in psychodrama. Chuck, remember how we helped you with your pain in the neck?"

Chuck was a member of my group B. He was one that had a warm smile. "Yeah doc, and I still work for that hard ass, but it is a little easier!"

Then Solomon turned to me. "Ellen, come up here and sit by me and we will talk a little about your headaches."

Dr. Nelson told me about this stuff. I found myself shuffling up to the stage with some curiosity and a lot of fear. Solomon quickly discovered that my last headache was yesterday. As usual, it was during a visit with Lucy. Solomon said that it was important to set the scene in detail, in my house where Lucy and I argued.

I remember picturing my living room and saying, "Now let me see … Here is the table, there is the sofa, my TV, a small bookshelf, and three of my elephants. Lucy was in the comfortable chair as usual and …"

Solomon interrupted me. "Tell me more about your elephants?" he curiously asked.

"That's not important," I said.

Solomon said that my face had softened and my neck was more relaxed looking when I mentioned the elephants—*my* elephants.

I stopped paying attention to the other patients like they were a hundred yards away. I explained to Solomon that I had 157 elephants. They were all over my house. They were made of stone, wood, metal, silver, gold, cut glass, crystal, plastic, and ivory. The one in the corner of my living room was four feet tall and had been carved by my father. He gave it to me for my nineteenth birthday and to celebrate my joining the navy. My dad was in the navy, too, and never forgot to bring me an elephant when he came back from a tour of duty. If he was gone on my birthday, he never forgot to mail me one special. I explained to Solomon that my dad died after my second year in the navy and right before Lucy was born.

Now it started to get weird and scary. Solomon set up chairs and tables like it was my house. He asked a nurse to play the role of Lucy. He asked one of the "Nam whiners" in my group to play my TV set. Solomon got my group buddy Chuck to play the four-foot wooden elephant in the corner.

The scene started with the TV news going. "Today, the president meets with his economic advisors about Medicare benefits. Later today, he will fly on Air Force One to ..."

The doorbell rang and it was Lucy." ... The west coast was hit by heavy rains, mudslides..." the news station continued to report. Then Lucy said with annoyance, "Mom, you can shut that damn TV off. It's always on so loud, and all the time here." (*It felt good when Solomon let me go over, turn the TV off, and shut up the Nam-whiner-turned-TV-set actor*).

I said, "I get lonely and you don't visit me much. The TV and my elephants are my only company. And, when you fuss at me I get a headache after you are here."

"Mom, your damn elephants are weird!" Lucy erupted. "It's embarrassing for me to even bring a friend with me. They're all over this small house. That big one over there is ugly and the oil you put on it smells!" (*My head was really hurting now*).

Chuck, who played the large wood elephant and with prompting whispers from Solomon, spoke up forcefully, "Ellen, tell Lucy who I am, *now!*" I burst into tears, then sobs.

Solomon froze the scene briefly and had two nursing students gently massage my tense neck and forehead. "Ellen, Lucy might or might not know the source of your elephants," Solomon explained, "but it seems clear that she doesn't know their deep and important meaning to you. Let's have you try to talk to Lucy about this."

Solomon had me repeatedly return to this scene in effort to help me talk to Lucy. Solomon had me reverse roles with Lucy, the wood elephant, and then back to myself again. I cried, I giggled, and I yelled at Lucy. I even pounded on a pillow named Lucy. (*A key prop at many psychodramas, I would later learn*).

The most moving part was when Chuck spoke in-role as the big wood elephant. He spoke gently but firmly directly to Lucy, "Lucy, in a real way I am your grandfather. My name is Carl and I loved your mother very much. You are your mom's only daughter, just like she was mine. You never knew me, because I died when you were very little."

I interrupted Chuck's soliloquy (*a big psychodrama word I learned*). "Lucy, I never wanted to burden you with all the grief about your grandpa," I said. "You know, I tried not to put all the hate of your dad on to you!"

The nurse in-role as Lucy said, "But Mom, I never knew these things. In fact, it seems like we never talk about anything important."

Now I was really boohooing hard. The group and Solomon were real respectful. They let me cry for quite a while. I told the group that my dad was wise and never forgot me.

"Like an elephant," someone gently said.

I went on to say that my dad had been too heavy, and his extra weight caused his early heart death. I'm also too heavy and feel blundering, lumbering, and have big sad ears and eyes. Only, I hear and see sad things.

Solomon suggested that we return to the scene to see what Lucy thought now. I took Lucy's role and the nurse playing my role asked, "So what would you like for us to talk about?"

I in Lucy's role suddenly said, "Roller skating. When I was little we used to go all the time. You could lose weight that way, Mom."

Then that crazy, gentle, silly, bastard Solomon had us move all the chairs near the walls. We all started to pretend to roller skate around and around the group room. A giggling Nam whiner played his harmonica to sound like organ music. Everyone was chuckling and crying, and I never have felt so close to a bunch of people since I was a little girl in church. I felt emotionally exhausted but my headache was gone!

Several mother/daughter family sessions helped the real Lucy and me to struggle to connect. After many months, and a bunch of roller skating time, I am a smaller but wiser elephant.

3

DOG-DAY IN PSYCHODRAMA
(A SHORT STORY)

*"Understanding the past in emotional depth, can
provide freedom from repeating its grasp."*

PAO

Julie knew she was a respected psychotherapist in her community. But, she never felt satisfied inside. After long days of helping others she often felt empty and sad. On her best days, Julie believed that her own inner demons helped her understand her clients. Most days, she knew that the distinction between therapists and patients was no more than an arbitrary spot on a vast human continuum.

Several nice men had been very interested in Julie over the years, and a couple of them had proposed marriage. But, the 'M-Word' terrified her. It would mean letting the man meet her family and see her humble origins. The men eventually ended the relationship. Often, they would comment that she was sweet but too serious. Damn that expression! "Too Serious!"

Before leaving her office, Julie noticed another weekend workshop on her schedule this weekend. She always had too many hours of continuing professional education each year. But, it made the weekends less long and lonely. This weekend's workshop was at Elm Tree Hospital.

John O'Neil and the group therapy department at Elm Tree Psychiatric Hospital had carefully planned and now looked forward to this weekend workshop with the world-famous psychodramatist, Zerka Moreno. They all sensed that this would not be a dry series of lectures. Zerka, the widow of J.L. Moreno who founded Psychodrama Treatment in 1910, is medium height, in her mid-sixties, and exudes barely contained energy and empathy. John briefly introduced Zerka to the sixty mental health professionals in attendance.

Moreno scanned the group with charismatic eye contact as she lectured briefly on the five classic phases of psychodrama; (1) Warm-up, (2) Setting the scene, (3) Rising Action, (4) Climax and (5) Audience group share-back. In a relaxed and clever way, Moreno had used the brief lecture as an effective warm-up technique and quickly plunged into a psychodrama.

Moreno said directly,

> "As therapists, you explore the childhood traumas of your patients. Don't cover-over your own childhood traumas by using therapy with your patients as a protective distraction. I want you to close your eyes and search within yourself for a painful unresolved traumatic event in your own childhood."

After five minutes, Moreno asked if anyone wanted to work on his or her trauma. Julie, felt slightly anxious, like before a high school girls' volleyball game. Yet, she timidly raised her hand. Julie felt safe with Moreno, and compelled onward by an inner almost mystic intuition. Moreno invited her to come up to the psychodrama stage. Moreno stood close to Julie and helped her describe her trauma in detail.

Julie described the small rural farm where she grew up. Julie brought the trauma scene to life as she talked about her hard-working but demanding and emotionally distant father. She was nine years old. She and her mother were sewing on the front porch. Her twelve-year-old brother Hank and her father were fixing a fence between the house and the dirt road fifty yards away. It was a scorching hot and dusty August Sunday afternoon.

Julie yelled to her beloved dog Hector as she carried his bowl with fresh cold water out in front of the porch. Hector raced happily across the road toward her wagging his tail. To Julie's sudden terror, a teenager in a red truck sped suddenly over the hill and struck Hector before speeding off in a cloud of dust. Hector limped, staggered and whimpered pitifully as he struggled to get to Julie. Hector listed to one side and his head and face were flooded with blood. Julie used her apron and the water to clean off blood as she cried and held Hector in her lap.

Julie's mother screamed,

> "Julie! That's your good dress and apron---you'll get them ruined with blood. Get away from Hector!"

Julie clung even harder to Hector and sobbed.

As her father and brother arrived, her father yelled.

> "Hank, get my rifle now, hurry!"

Julie's father yanked her away from Hector roughly, and Hector growled at him. Hector began to run around in close staggering circles. Then he began to have epileptic seizures and defecate. Her mother and brother held Julie and complained of the foul smell. Julie clawed and fought to reach Hector who had whimpered and lay still after the seizure Without a word Julie's father shot Hector in the head and began to drag his lifeless, bloody body toward the back pasture for burial. Julie sobbed for hours. She finally cried herself to sleep as she clung to her stuffed dog.

The next morning her father helped Julie make a cross and pick flowers for Hector's grave. But, there was not much meaningful conversation.

Moreno gently helped a tearful Julie pick people from the audience to play her father, mother and brother. Then came the choice of who would play Hector and Julie picked John. She always felt envious and competitive towards John but she sensed that he had a good soul.

John's inner thoughts whirled chaotically as he loosened his tie, took off his jacket and headed to the stage. John thought to himself, "A stupid, bleeding, epileptic dog! All these mental health colleagues are probably already chuckling under their breath at Julie's choice of me for the part. Hey, wait a minute!! I can't fail Julie now. I am a therapist, a physician, and a psychiatrist. Get a hold of your empathy and compassion John! You're a Doctor! Stop acting like a veterinarian's patient."

The psychodrama proceeded in a powerful and poignant way. At his cue, John scampered on all fours across the road. The imagined red truck smacked him down. Wounded, he struggled towards Julie with his best dog whimper, and she held John/Hector bleeding in her arms. John's suit got dusty, stretched and wrinkled as he crawled tripping and whimpering in pitiful circles. John growled and snapped at Julie's father when he grabbed her roughly. John convulsed and lay in his imagined psychodrama blood and feces as Hank and Julie's mother complained of his smell. John then lay still as Julie's father shot him in the head and dragged him off stage. More dust and wrinkles for his suit.

Moreno helped Julie vent her rage at her father by creating a new scene where she confronted him with her current thirty-year-old woman's articulateness. Julie also pounded on a hospital-owned Gym mat until she was exhausted. She screamed at her mother for the shallowness of her concern about blood-soiled clothes to the exclusion of empathy for Julie's feelings about Hector. Julie's brow was covered with perspiration.

In an imagined scene suggested by someone in the audience, Julie and her psychodrama father went to confront the careless teenage driver and his parents. Damn those hormone-driven teenage boy drivers that drive too fast!

Audience members shared experiences about traumatic losses of pets during their own childhoods. Moreno liked that. She said that it is a mistake in psychodrama technique to allow the audience to just analyze from a distance about the protagonist's "Problems". Julie felt safe in this large group like she had never felt at a workshop before.

Moreno said that it is more therapeutic for everyone if the finale of the psychodrama is truly a "Share-back" and not just 'clinical' feedback.

Moreno hugged Julie and asked how she was doing. Julie confirmed that she was slowly decompressing psychologically from her psychodrama experience during the 'share-back'. She felt relief and a sense of mastery over 'old painfulness and helplessness'. She said that this psychodrama had been one of the most meaningful events in her life. The pain had been cooped-up too long! She thanked Moreno and the group. She smiled warmly at John.

Everyone experienced the benevolent power and value of skillfully conducted psychodrama on that "Dog Day". Julie and John will certainly never forget the experience. Each time she sees John at a meeting, Julie pats him on the head and says, "Good Dog".

4

THERAPEUTIC GRIEF OVER A STILLBORN BABY BOY AT PSYCHODRAMA

(The challenge of role-playing a still born baby of a heroin addict.)

Amber is a strikingly beautiful blonde woman. She was admitted to our inpatient service for depression, severe heroin addiction, and serious suicidal urges. Amber's therapist urged her to present her situation at our weekly psychodrama group.

Tony Andrews is a talented musician and doctor of internal medicine. He is interested in the subspecialty of addiction medicine. Tony and I did a weekly psychodrama group together for acutely hospitalized psychiatric patients. Many have alcohol and or substance abuse problems.

Tony is five- feet- ten, slender and physically fit. He has red-brown graying hair, a ready smile, and impressive objective empathy for patients.

Today, Tony is directing the psychodrama. Amber anxiously requests work on her problems. Her hands tremble. Her voice hesitating, her face sad. Tony asks her to join him on the psychodrama stage area. They sit side-by-side as Terry warms the group up with banter and jokes about a frequent topic, hospital cuisine.

Tony asks Amber,

"What would you like us to work on Amber?"

Amber tears-up saying,

"I killed him. I murdered my own little boy"

A tense hush hit our psychodrama audience group. For minutes that seemed like hours, Amber sobbed. She then told her story quietly, interspersed by sobs.

She had been so heavy into heroin that her ex-husband took custody of her two young children. Amber's widowed mother allowed her to stay at her apartment in lieu of the streets. Though not clearly showing, Amber knew she was at least twenty weeks pregnant. She had found an NA romance partner soon after her last attempt at sobriety. They both relapsed deeper into heroin. Her partner died of an overdose. Amber didn't know for sure who her baby's father was. She had unprotected sex while doing tricks to get money for she and her now dead partner.

Early one morning Amber awoke with labor pains and before long delivered a tiny baby boy. He cried weakly, gasped, struggled to breath briefly, then, fell silent. Amber quietly cleaned-up, went out to a dumpster where she threw her dead barely born baby. Amber was sobbing and named her dead baby Paul. Amber's mother awoke to find Amber bleeding profusely from slashed wrists. She took her severely depressed daughter to the hospital.

Tony helped Amber set the scene for us in the spare bedroom at her mother's apartment. At the appropriately timed moment Tony directed me to play Amber's new born baby struggling for breath. I dramatized the gasping, crying baby as best I could. I abruptly said to Amber,

"Mom, help me. Help me, I don't want to die! I'm little,
my life won't be lived. I could have had your love if

Heroin wasn't your lover. I'll never live to see my own babies. Mommy, how could you?"

I then gasped and played a lifeless baby. Amber sobbed for a time while holding my head in her lap. As Tony had her toss me in the dumpster, I collapsed in the corner of the stage unmoving. Then Tony suddenly shifted the scene saying,

"Amber, though this never happened, I want us to have a symbolic funeral for little Paul."

Tony had me stretch out on three chairs my body cushioned by three pillows. Another patient Harold offered to play the role of the priest. Harold had been a chaplain in the Navy where his severe alcoholism had its beginnings. Tony asked to come back briefly from the land of the dead. I said,

"Mom, I forgive you. God forgives you because you are getting treatment for your Heroin addiction. Remember my short life by getting yours back. Don't go back to the Heroin death world. Make my memory special by forgiving yourself. Save yourself and God and I will remember."

The whole psychodrama group entered a quiet hush as Amber sobbed. A nurse offered her a Kleenex. Two women fellow patients came up from the audience to hug Amber. Another patient shared her own experience of guilt and now grief over getting an abortion during her long time of Heroin addiction. After many years of sobriety, she felt her continuing depression was related to the abortion and the marriage she lost due to her addiction. She cried and hugged Amber.

The small groups on the psychiatry unit and individual therapy sessions actively followed up on the theme of that psychodrama.

Working through of Amber's guilt, grief and eventual mourning process took many months prior to her discharge from the hospital. I saw Amber a year after discharge as I was leaving the hospital one evening. She was having a cup of coffee after an aftercare group she had been attending at the hospital. She came up and hugged me saying,

> "I often think of you as my little Paul might have been,
> all grown-up. I am a day-at-a-time sober now for over
> a year. I work as a teacher aid at a private preschool. I
> love my kids. Thank you, little big Paul."

We smiled at each other with the smile that sometimes hard work in therapy brings.

5

A NARRATOR AND THREE FOXHOLES AT PSYCHODRAMA

The VA Day hospital is an exciting and scary place to work lately.

I work as a consultant to the small groups and direct the psychodrama therapy every Friday morning from 10:00 to 11;30. This is a valuable teaching experience for the young psychologists, psychiatry residents and social work students. Our supervision hour at 9:00 each Friday allows for the pulse to be taken about the atmosphere in the day hospital large group. The several small groups led by cotherapists describe active individual patient issues. Some problems individuals raise in their individual therapy sessions can be worked on in the psychodrama session. Psychodrama is attended by all patients and staff at the day hospital.

Currently, the day hospital census is full with a waiting list. The Vietnam war is winding down and many depressed, paranoid and angry young men are being admitted. They don't come out and say it, but the United States lost the war. The defeat and its implications threaten the very soul of a proud but spiritually bloodied America. The war wounded souls are widespread throughout America's entire population. The pain is particularly acute among our young Nam veteran patients who are not greeted with pride and gratitude like the WWII vets received in their day. Some have even been booed or insulted as "Killers" by their community. The Korean war vets fall in between the derision and pity the Nam vets get on their return to the country and the pride felt by the WWII vets.

Our depressed young Nam patients are mingled in with crusty old WWII veterans and middle- aged Korean war vets. Tension is building between the three groups. Several fist fights had to be broken-up by staff.

At today's warm-up to psychodrama I raise the issue of tension between the three groups directly. At first the group tries to brush off the issue. One rigid WWII army vet says,

> "Doc the problem is these young wet-behind- the- ears
> kids just whine and bitch. That uses up group time."

A Nam vet exploded,

> "You old fart. You don't know what it's f-ing…. like!"

I had a sudden inspiration. I pictured three foxholes. One in Nam, one in in Okinawa, and one in South Korea. It was going to be tough. But, as director I made my decision saying,

> "OK guys, today we are goanna have three foxholes
> here on the stage. One for Nam, one for Okinawa and
> one for South Korea. I want two volunteers for each.
> We are going to try to get to listen and hear what each
> fox hole is like. It's hard, but we want to listen not talk
> at each other. Dr. Stan will be like Walter Cronkite. I
> want him to stand up on a chair and from time to time
> comment like a TV broadcast about what is going on
> in our foxholes".

I knew Stan James was very verbal and knowledgeable about military history.

I directed the representatives from each war to situate their foxholes in three distinct spots on the stage. I asked the Korean vets to start helping us with the Korea conditions. A gray -haired Sargent with a crew cut began gruffly,

> "It's damn cold here. I can hardly feel my fingers. How the hell can I fire my gun when I must. How can I even take a shit or a piss here in this frozen hole? I'm scared shitless. Those Chinese commies can come charging at us all-of -a-sudden. The guy on watch better stay wake. Man, I can't sleep."

Stan James boomed his best Walter Cronkite voice saying,

> "Seems like a long time ago Korea. A U.N. police action, they called it"

Sargent crew cut boomed,

> Shit, it don't matter what they call this kind of frozen hell. I want a warm bath, a clean warm bed and a hot whore..."

Sarge's foxhole buddies agreed ...even recalled names of favorite whores.

I asked the Nam vets to describe their foxhole. It took some time before a burley red-bearded vet with long hair took the leap saying,

> "It's f...en hot, humid and I know I stink. My crotch rot is so bad my balls hurt and itch. If I scratch em it gets worse. The damn jungle's so thick and who knows when a snake will bite my ass. The gooks make noises out there in the dark. It's hard to tell gooks from animals crashing

around. I don't think our Lieutenant knows where we are. He seems scared of us but bosses us around bad. I got four more months in this shit hole and I'm outa here. What's my girl doing at home? We don't get letters often. At home, I hear lots of people hate our being here. No one cares. The politicians are running things stupidly. They don't give a damn about us grunts over here. That damn Joan Baez and Jane Fonda came here to call us baby killers and war criminals at concerts here as we were being shot at doing our duty. Our guys get booed and spit-on when they get home."

Stan commented more quietly now,

"Lonely, scared and bitter. A bad mixture in a war damned by politicians' ambitions and stupidity."

Dr. Stan now boomed out,

"Two foxholes reported, where's the third?"

A frail looking white-haired man in a baseball cap inscribed "WWII VET" leaned on his cane saying,

"You Vietnam Vets think you had hot sweaty conditions. Try the Philippine Islands' forms of jungle rot. They had funguses there that stank so much I could hardly stand my own smell. Them Japs were so cruel we heard that it seemed like we never slept out of fear they might jump us at night. And walking the point of the platoon patrol got this white hair of mine started when I was nineteen. You young Turks ever heard of the Batten Death March? Read about it before you bitch about the Viet Cong gooks."

Veterans from each of the three foxholes began describing in detail the trials and tribulations they each went through. The jibes and peculiar forms of bragging about their miseries and maladies began to get intense. A "can-you-top-this" quality of competitive dueling descriptions

As director, I then suddenly started reversing roles of the three foxholes. I had the patients swap hats as they changed foxholes on the psychodrama stage. In remarkable detail, they threw back accurate elements of each other's ordeals. Occasionally with humor, often with a sad realization of things experienced in common the emotional tone shifted more to one of empathy and sharing.

Dr. Stan from his perch standing above the scene on his chair said solemnly,

> "Brave, tired and scared men in three foxholes find some common ground. Three different eras, three different climates in both weather and climate for homecomings. No apologies for bitterness and resentment of distant political authorities issuing orders from safe spots far from the pain and blood. A brotherhood found in the fight to survive and have each other's backs."

After a hush in the group. I began to lead the feedback (Share-back). The war stories on stage triggered discussion from the all- important audience group of veterans. They shared some of their own war experiences but importantly connected the impact of the combat PTSD and heavy burden of stored-up emotions on their current life situations. The impact of war horror memories on current jobs, marital and home life was discussed. One young Nam Vet said,

> "I sit in the evening sipping a beer and watching my little kids play. I think those *lucky little shits. Why can't I relax and have fun with them?*"

Another vet who described bloody flashbacks from freezing trenches of hand- to- hand fighting in Korea said,

> "Yeah son, I felt like home life after the war was boring and dull. Empty. I never felt so scared shitless but so alive I felt, heard my saw my bayonet flashing and doing its work. Over and over again. My wife got real scared of my flashbacks. We even got up and walked around the block in the middle of the night sometimes."

After the conclusion of that psychodrama the small groups and further psychodrama therapy sessions showed significantly better group cohesiveness, genuine sharing and helping each other with problems. "Those damn three foxholes" came up frequently in discussions at the day hospital. They became a helpful symbol of a therapeutic brotherhood.

6

PSYCHODRAMA WITH HEROIN ADDICTS RETURNING FROM DUTY IN VIETNAM

Shortly after reporting for duty at Oakland Naval Hospital I learned I was to be the medical officer in charge of a newly established psychiatric unit for substance abuse patients retuning to the United States from duty in Vietnam. Psychodrama therapy became an integral part of our evaluation and treatment program.

Perry is a nineteen-year-old man seriously addicted to heroin. Perry tried to quit on his own but could not. A positive urine drug test made his entry into the drug amnesty program imperative. Three weeks after detox on our unit Perry presented to our psychodrama group in an acutely distressed state. He was pale, sweating, restless and extremely anxious and fearful. His urine had been clean for opiates and he did not have cramping or goose flesh typical of physical withdrawal. Perry told the group he had a dreadful dream the night before.

Perry's dream was brought to life on the psychodrama stage. In the dream, he had been discharged from the Navy to return home. At the front door of his house in Detroit he was confronted by his angry father. A staff member played Perry's angry father. The father-son confrontation escalated and violent threats occurred. As director, I stopped the action and asked the patient to reverse roles with his father. I asked him to guess what his father was thinking. Perry said,

> "This damn son of mine is just like my kid sister. Love
> was not enough to stop her heroin addiction. Susie
> tried to kick her heroin habit several times. She died
> of suicide alone and unknown in a far-off city. I am so
> mad at my son I could kick his butt."

Perry looked stunned with a realization.

The next and final scene of Perry's psychodrama took place as the dream images took place in his thirteen-year-old brother's room. Kid brother Ben had always idolized and looked up to Perry. Perry had always tried to discourage Ben from drug use. Perry had recently learned in a letter from Ben's close friend that Ben was now addicted to heroin.

Now in the psychodrama enacted dream Perry was in his brother's room to try to talk sense to him about quitting heroin. Suddenly in the dream, while Perry was talking to Ben the dream scene shifted again and he and Ben were injecting heroin together with the same needle. "Oh, no, it can't be!" Perry gasped. The last scene had abruptly ended early that morning when Perry awoke in a cold sweat. He awakened a buddy on our unit to tell him about the dream.

As director, I sat next to Perry on the stage as he proceeded with a guilt-laden soliloquy about his dream and its meaning. The spellbound audience of fellow heroin addicts struggled with words of empathic and supportive feedback. Perry realized that part of his father's extreme anger at any hints of drug abuse was related to his father's pain and agony about the memory of his sister's tragic demise from heroin. Perry always assumed that his dad merely inherently disliked Perry. Some audience group members pointed out that Perry had been a bad example and partially responsible for Ben's heroin use. But there were other factors as well. It was tough enough for Perry to kick his own heroin habit, much less heap Ben's problem on Perry's already sagging shoulders.

A fellow patient astutely observed for himself and for Perry that the upsetting dream best be used now on the treatment unit to help face their problems than at home later, alone and vulnerable to a relapse.

On the unit on subsequent days Perry seemed relieved, more relaxed and motivated for further therapy. Additional psychodrama sessions were used by Perry to rehearse his dealing with his father and brother when he was home after discharge from the navy.

Such dream's as Perry's came to life at psychodramas on our unit. The dreams become a therapeutic opportunity for the entire community of heroin addicts. Better in dreams enacted in therapy than stored-up nightmares in the oblivion of things unmentioned.

Nineteen -year-old **Mac** stopped heroin three weeks ago as he arrived on our unit. He had used heroin for a year previously. Mac's father is a hard worker who is loving and caring towards Mac. Part of their close father son relationship was hunting together. His father taught Mac great car of and safe use of guns. Mac's father was stern and meticulous about gun care and safety.

At the warm-up phase of Mac's psychodrama, I as director was involved in light banter with the audience over the usual topics of sea stories about heroin use and rebellious statements about military authority. I had found that such banter was a test of me as an authority. I tolerated such banter as a warm-up activity. I noticed Mac was seating, shaky, shifting positions, and holding his head in his hands. I asked and Mac said, "I don't feel good but I got to tell you and the community about my dream last night." The dream had awoken Mac abruptly.

A lengthy soliloquy by Mac helped set up the dream scene in detail. Mac and his beloved father were deer hunting. Mac found himself looking through the telescopic sight of a deer rifle. To his abject horror, Mac saw the smiling face of his best childhood friend in the crosshairs. Mac was unable to stop as he relentlessly squeezed the trigger of the powerful weapon. The shot struck his best friend in the left chest. In the heart! Another second shot in his friend's groin. Mac's tears filled his eyes. Astounding to Mac was the twisted but clearly ecstatic smile of his friend who was transfixed in the rifle scope. Mac said, "It was almost sexual doc."

Role reversals and further soliloquy with returns to the scene with doubling to expose Mac's unconscious feelings helped to clarify Mac's feelings. During the "love-back of audience feedback a perceptive fellow patient observed with striking clarity, "It takes no shrink to see that best friend of yours is really you man! Each time you shoot up heroin, you shoot up yourself. Another patient described his girlfriend's ecstatic smile as she shot up heroin with him. Our psychologist pointed out to Mac that the bullet in the groin as well as the heart fit in with recent ward lectures by a physician who described cardiac and sexual complications associated with IV drug abuse. Mac had been in fact impotent during his chronic heavy heroin use. His girlfriend had gotten SDT while prostituting for money to support her habit. Mac expressed gratitude for the help he got from the psychodrama therapy group. He in turn helped other patients in their work on issues in their lives brought to life at psychodrama. Mac commented often that helping others at their psychodramas helped him maintain strength about his sobriety.

Discussion:

In the active small groups and psychodrama group therapy sessions in our hospital program we found ourselves talking to patients about "turning on to life" or seeking a "natural high". The abuser of marijuana, hallucinogens or heroin first chose to enter an Alice-in-Wonderland or soothing world. Then over time they habitually seek refuge in the vivid, but artificial land of the trip or the rush. In time, they find the everyday experience of living a blur or boring. Our treatment team has sought ways to jolt the young addicts from their tragic world of self-induced anesthesia to life back to reality. We sought to help them substitute a healthy addiction for a destructive one. Heroin is hopefully replaced by addiction to creative experiences in living with people.

The cornerstones of psychodrama theory described by Moreno 1964), came into vital focus in our treatment endeavors with heroin addicts. Moreno talked about spontaneity and creativity in living. Moreno said we call response to a new problem situation with ancient ways of wisdom and, a new creative response to an old habitual situation---spontaneity. Spontaneity Moreno said is the factor animating all psychic phenomenon to appear fresh, new and flexible. It gives situations the quality of momentariness (without drugs) … With a total loss of spontaneity goes a total loss of creative existence.

Young heroin addicts because of their retreat into the drug haze are in fact rigid, despite their youthful age. Psychodrama treatment can provide an opportunity to turn on to life, not slow death. At a, less theoretical level psychodrama is useful. Very practical life situations can be vividly and helpfully approached via the psychodrama stage. We found that military duty situations, future job situations, and home, marital and family situations could be set up on stage to be looked at and dealt with in new and creative ways. We hoped there would be a psychological desensitization to future stressful situations to avoid the return to heroin use. With one young sailor, we staged his return home to confess to his heroin addiction and recovery process to his wife. His unknowing wife had been waiting patiently for him at home. Her tears, anger and fear pervaded the stage as we helped him prepare for the event at his homecoming.

As a fellow patient said that day, "Even though this psychodrama upset you man, it is better for you face that stuff here and now on the unit." To face it later at home alone without preparation might be too much to face without return to heroin."

On our heroin addiction treatment unit, we found that "Acting-in" at psychodrama reduced acting-out behaviors on our unit. Hopefully the long- term impact of creative action in psychodrama helped patients maintain their sobriety after discharge from the military or back at a duty station. Letters we received from former patients supported that hope. Military life helps many young men work through their authority conflicts. Many of our patients for various reasons however had intense anger and bitterness towards the military and American society in general. This appeared to involve what Gruenberg called a negative transference towards an institution. Because the military is perceived as an agent of discipline and real authority as well as a total care institution (Providing food, clothing, pay and shelter), it tends to rekindle buried or smoldering conflicts with parents. In a significant number of cases a parent had been directly, vicariously, or indirectly involved with substance abuse. The alcoholic parent seemed to be the most frequent depicted at psychodrama sessions. But, a parent as a physician, pharmacist, drug salesman or drug store clerk walked our psychodrama stage at therapy sessions. Many substance abusers start out at their parent's medicine cabinets or home liquor cabinets.

Unfeeling, unjust discipline is occasionally found in the military. This sad abuse of power usually comes from those who feel inadequate and use the system of military discipline for their own psychological security operations. As we explored such situations at psychodramas we often found that behind such hassles with authority were disguised remnants of either cruel, uncaring, rigid or uncaringly permissive experiences with parents or perceived as such. Thus, the military is hated or rebelled against or paradoxically sought after to set limits or to care as parents were not experienced helpful in that way. Those who successfully found the good parent in the military we rarely encountered on the unit.

In summary, we found the psychodrama stage to be a diagnostic clinical laboratory par excellence. We found that in psychodrama we could know our patients' worlds as they really are. "Show us don't tell us!" and "You are there right now" were common reminders we gave to our patients during psychodrama sessions. Many of our patients were impulsive actors rather than verbalizers. Those of us involved with psychodrama for our young heroin addicts will never be the same for it.

7

PEDAGOGIC DRAMA AND POETRY THERAPY

Trying to Practice What You Teach

It is idiomatic that teachers and preachers should practice what they teach and preach. Two of my recent teaching experiences have had strong impact upon me. While teaching a course in basic psychopathology for lay therapists (Irvin A. Kraft's N. T. T. program, i.e. new traditional therapists), I struggled to try to present material in a vivid manner. These therapists would be seeing real live persons and even if adequately supervised, the anxiety for the teacher-supervisor was great! All the subtly ingrained concerns emanating from my medical psychiatric training impinged on me. "Could they do it?"

My trainees were bright, some of them extremely creative, rich in life's experiences, and many had long experience with children of their own. However, did they know of "real medical responsibility?" Had they been there at birth and death, pain and suffering? All these considerations bombarded me as I prepared for the course. As it occurred to me that these lay therapists would soon be seeing children, mothers, fathers, and families, I struggled to try to present material in a striking way, so that they could capture a sense of what it was really like for the patients in their to-and-fro journey towards help. Clinical vignettes in the textbooks were cogent, but they did not convey the personal sense of involvement and anxiety experienced by a mother bringing her child, by a family coming with fear of their hidden secrets or a couple with their hates and loves. My idea was to have class members rewrite the cases as presented in the child psychiatry and adult psychiatry textbooks in terms of a literary rewriting of the case history by the student. The student was to place himself in the shoes and hopefully the skin of the presenting patient. They were told to let their fantasies run free and describe what it would be like for themselves to present with a problem to the clinic.

Next the trainees role-played their patient presentations in front of our teaching-supervision group. The results were striking in terms of the trainee's productive learning and the lessening of my anxiety as their psychotherapy supervisor. Trainees felt this pedagogic drama helped build their objective empathy toward our clinic patients and added to their diagnostic skills.

Next, I will present a clinical teaching situation from the viewpoint of myself the teacher; from the patient's viewpoint, as profound yet unaware teacher; and then my poetic reaction to the experience.

My Doctor-Teacher's Experience with Emily

Patients have always been recognized as our best teachers in psychiatry and the psychotherapies. Recently, I had been asked to lecture on psychodrama techniques at a state mental hospital in another state. When I wrote to the Director of Education and asked if a patient population could be present at the latter part of both the morning and afternoon session for teaching purposes, he stated that it was against the law in that state for patients to be used for demonstration. Conditions on the ward, the emphasis on medication only, and the somewhat apathetic attitude that had developed regarding talking techniques of therapy was a problem.

The patient encounter described next had the impact of being a most profound example of psychotherapeutic pedagogy. In a simple, but most poignant way, this patient had helped myself and the staff of that hospital to understand in a most vivid way the human techniques of contact that never will be replaced by the most sophisticated chemical and pharmacologic solutions to mental problems.

So, I had geared myself towards using staff participants in the conference to demonstrate the psychodrama and role-playing techniques that I had planned to discuss in the didactic portion of my presentation.

My lecture was held in the chapel at the state hospital. Midway in the morning of my talk, I was approaching the end of the lecture portion of the program. I was, at that point, contemplating how I would mobilize some of the staff to participate in the demonstration aspect of the psychodrama. I began to ask the staff to think of patient problem situations on their own ward or clinic area that we could then look at in some psychodrama demonstrations.

At that very moment, a patient walked through the rear doors of the chapel and proceeded to walk up the center aisle. She had long, stringy hair, was about forty years of age, and walked slowly up the aisle glancing at the various stained-glass windows and ornaments of the chapel. She was singing a hymn in low monotone and fondling various small flowers with which she had adorned her hair. When she glanced up and saw my long-haired presence at the lectern, she stated, "Oh, Jesus, can you help me?" I responded to her by saying, "I'm Dr. Olsson. I'd like to try to help you. Can you come up and we can talk."?

We both sat together on the platform and she introduced herself as Emily. "Emily," I said, "What seems to be the trouble?" She said, "My nurse won't listen to me or talk to me." She went on to describe how her nurse, whose name was Annie, would not listen to her in the morning. She said that the nurse would say, "Take your Thora zine, take your Thora zine," but never would sit and talk with her. I asked Emily if she would mind helping us to look at that situation by pretending we were on her ward, and I asked one of the nurses in the audience to participate as her nurse named Annie. The nurse picked up on the psychodrama technique and said, "Emily, take your Thora zine, take your Thora zine!" Emily said, "But I want to talk, I want to talk!"

I then did a role reversal and explained to Emily that she was now Annie, her nurse. She walked over to the nurse (who was now playing her), put her arm around the nurse's shoulder and said, "Emily, you look so sad this morning. Let's sit down and talk for a little while." At that point, I again reversed roles, explaining to Emily that she was herself again. She seemed to be having fun and then said, "My sister says she is such a good Christian, but every week for six weeks now, she's said she would bring my children to visit me, but they never come! Every Saturday morning, I sit, and it's eight o'clock, nine o'clock, ten o'clock, eleven o'clock and my children never come and see me." At that point Emily burst into sudden tears of anger and sadness. The nurse then grasped the situation and said, "Emily, we'll have to try to contact our social worker and have her call your sister and see why it is that she isn't able to bring your children. We'll try to do our best to see that she brings your children to see you." Emily then said, "Thank you very much, oh, thank you! I hope you can help me with that."

I then said to Emily, "Thank you very much for helping us this morning. We hope you're feeling better, Emily."

She said, "Thank you, Jesus, thank you," and proceeded at her slow pace along the far side of the chapel out towards the back door singing, glancing at the stained -glass windows, and then disappeared back toward her hospital ward of loneliness.

Emily's Psychodrama Experience Imagined

It was one of those windy, but warm early spring days that everyone knows about and most people enjoy. Today is Friday. Will tomorrow be the usual eight o'clock, nine o'clock, ten o'clock, nothing? Are those tears I feel? Yes, I've waited six weeks and each passing Saturday to see the smiling faces of those little ones I love. The voices say, "Kill the bitch! She says she's religious!" "Your own sister! Ha ha!" Those voices used to scare me so, but now they only hurt. They hurt with the dreadfully certain truth that I have not seen my children in six weeks. My, the wind is blowing hard. I'm just about at the chapel. The chapel finds my heart in a special way. I can sing there. I can pray there. Maybe someone, maybe God, will hear. I love those stained-glass windows. They say things to me that people don't seem to be able to say. What are all the people doing in here? The chapel is for praying, but that man is talking. Is it a service? I guess I better sing. "Rock of Ages, cleft for me. Wait a minute, that man has long hair, a quiet gentle face. He's talking in such an understanding way. "Jesus, can you help me?" (Is it Him?) He said his name but I couldn't hear it. He's asking me to come and talk. I seldom talk, but his eyes say it's okay. I wish I could have talked to the nurse this morning. She sometimes seems to care. I found myself saying, "I have trouble because my nurse won't listen to me." Actually no one listens to me. No one takes me seriously. The voices say, "Ha ha! No one listens. No one hears you, you fool!" Yet, that quiet voice. He wants me to do something. Talk to my nurse? Here, up on the platform? So silly! But his voice sounds calm and quiet. Oh well! What's that nurse doing, coming up from the audience? Oh, she will be my nurse? She's telling me to take that Thorazine again. I hate for them always to say, "Take medicine, take medicine, Emily!" What is Jesus saying? He's saying for me to be my nurse? How can that be? But it's fun, kind of like a game. I'll show the nurse; I'll go over and hold her. "Oh, Emily, you look so sad this morning. Let's talk for a while." It feels good saying those words, just in the very saying of the words. Now he wants me to change back? Be me? The voices say, "How silly! Won't help! No! Bad! Dangerous!" I'm telling her about my sister. This nurse seems to hear me. She seems interested. Maybe what she says about the social worker might come true. There was that one social worker . . . she did help. Toothpaste, toothbrush, that towel, some clothes. Sometimes they help. He's gently telling me to go now. Gee! The stained- glass windows and the pictures are so pretty! This is a peaceful place. We used to sing a hymn as we left the church. "Rock of Ages, cleft for me. . Let me hide myself in Thee." Better say something. Turn around, look at him. "Thank you, Jesus." I wonder if I'll see my children tomorrow?

Emily had helped myself and the staff of that hospital to understand in a most vivid way the human techniques of contact that never will be replaced by the most sophisticated chemical and pharmacologic solutions to mental problems.

We thank you, Emily, for your day as our teacher.

*Portions of this account about Emily appeared in VOICES: Journal of the American Academy of Psychotherapists Summer, 1975 pp28-31.

8

MEDICAL STUDENT TEACHING AND PEDAGOGIC DRAMA

When I was teaching at Baylor College of Medicine Alex Pokorny chief of psychiatry and Joe Merrill professor of medicine asked me to do some psychodrama sessions with Baylor medical students on their rehab medicine clerkship. I was supposed to try to teach them about empathy. One session I had them all be blind folded and find their way around the building and back to our lecture room. At the next session, I had them plug their ears and try to give slightly complicated directions to a partner as if they were trying to convey and understand a range of motion exercise prescription. At the next session, the students all bound up their knees, elbows and hands tightly to represent significant arthritis. They then went to the halls for a lengthy walk with a task of opening a heavy door at the end of their trek. At the final session, we listened to a partner's heart and lungs with the students' eyes closed. An ice cube made the stethoscope very cold which made the point of warming stethoscopes before clinical application.

Joe Merrill did statistical analysis of the groups over two years as to their degree of empathy on a scale he had devised. One group had our psychodrama sessions, a control group had the regular teaching rotation without psychodrama. The student groups that had the psychodrama did significantly better in empathy from the control.

9

THE USE OF PEDAGOGIC DRAMA
IN PSYCHIATRIC EDUCATION
OF MEDICAL STUDENTS

A faculty colleague of mine at Baylor and I were asked to give several lectures to medical students about anxiety disorder, obsessive-compulsive disorder and depression by a senior faculty professor of psychiatry. Several days before our series of lectures we learned that the patients from the professor's private practice scheduled for interviews with us in front of the med students had refused the interviews. Rather than dry didactic lectures we decided that one of us would role-play the patient with a student asked to interview us. We prepared carefully so our simulated patients would display important verbal and non- verbal diagnostic clues.

The presentations went well. In fact, at the first class several med students came late to class and chided their colleagues in the class for laughing out loud at the patient. At their semester examinations, the students did consistently well on test questions about anxiety disorder, obsessive compulsive disorder, and depression.

One feature of pedagogic drama that was helpful to the students' learning was for them to reverse roles with the simulated patient and to have several students try their role as the interviewer. We used instant replays to suggest changes in their interview technique. The teaching session were lively and no students fell asleep as some might do at traditional lectures.

Reference:
Byrd, G and Olsson, P "The Use of Pedagogic Drama in Psychiatric Education". *Journal of Medical Education.* Vol 50, March 1975.

10

APPLICATIONS OF PSYCHODRAMA AND PEDAGOGIC DRAMA TO TEACHING AND SUPERVISION OF PSYCHOTHERAPISTS

It is often helpful at individual psychotherapy supervision to have the trainee enact his patient's verbal and non-verbal behavior at a recent session. The supervisor needs to listen and observe carefully to the trainee's descriptions of therapy sessions before possible blind-spots can be spotted. Then the direct exchange with the thusly dramatized patient can help the trainee to learn to deal with patient defenses and dysfunctional behaviors or personality styles.

Pedagogic drama techniques can be used effectively to teach students of group and family therapy to portray dysfunctional couples, families and individual patient behavior problems arising in therapy groups. These applications of pedagogic drama require careful preparation which also stimulates students and teachers to read the psychodynamic and group dynamic literature as preparation. Trainees also learn to improve their interview and psychotherapeutic style and technique. Some teaching centers have used professional actors and actresses to act-out problem behaviors. Some of the most dramatic portrayals for study are the handling of the acutely suicidal, homicidal, assaultive or psychotic patient in the therapy group.

COTHERAPY PROBLEMS and PSYCHODRAMA

In supervising co-therapists of group or family therapy can be helped and enlivened by role-plying techniques. Co-therapist conflicts, techniques used with problem patients, over-identification with patients, and sub-grouping events can come under helpful scrutiny via role-playing and pedagogic drama.

SUPERVISION of GROUP PSYCHOTHERAPY via PEDAGOGIC PSYCHODRAMA

In this approach group therapists or co-therapists in training attend a pedagogic psychodrama group each week instead of taking process notes or videotapes to individual sessions with supervisors. This has the following benefits: (1) Recreation of impasse situations and severe resistances in the group being supervised; (2) Countertransference phenomena can be brought into focus by enacting family-of-origin scenes from the therapist's own family that act as a resistance within the therapist toward doing the therapeutic work; (3) Co-therapy communication problems, theoretical orientation differences and conflicts between therapists' interpretive approaches can be delved into in a hopefully neutral way at pedagogic drama. This requires maturity and courage in both therapists and supervisors. The group therapists not on focus on such events in the group supervisory hour can serve as auxiliaries in the pedagogic enactment of the group therapy session being processed and studied; (4) Simulated groups can be used in didactic presentations of the various group therapy theoretical approaches (psychoanalytic, experiential, gestalt, transactional analysis, Jungian etc.); (5) Cathartic pedagogic drama can be used to resolve therapist "burn-out" and inter-professional tensions about theoretical issues in the learning group.(Physicians, psychologists, social workers, nurses).

11

PEDAGOGIC DRAMA IN A GROUP PSYCHOTHERAPY TRAINING PROGRAM

The faculty at the Houston Group Psychotherapy Association's training program felt that psychiatric diagnostic skills are important in screening potential therapy group members, in assessing the progress made by group members and in the performance of the complex leadership responsibility in leading a therapy group. An effective psychotherapist not only confirms diagnoses but tries to aid and facilitate positive changes in the diagnoses and conflicts of group members by the impact of a well-led group therapy process. Formal lectures on the topic of psychopathology can be dry and boring but the following teaching procedure was found to enliven the teaching of psychiatric diagnosis to group psychotherapy students of all mental health disciplines.

Each of the twenty group therapy students in the class was asked to spend ample time studying, reviewing, and thinking about descriptive psychiatric diagnoses. These study efforts provided raw material for each student's preparation for their detailed role-played portrayal of a patient being considered for group psychotherapy. At two consecutive weeks' sessions, a volunteer male and female students were asked to play the part of a co-therapy team preparing to start a private practice, six to eight-member outpatient, weekly, insight-oriented, open-ended diagnostically heterogeneous therapy group.

The role-played planning session for the group proved valuable in high-lighting co-therapy dilemmas even before their first group session occurred. Whose office would be used? Would they interview prospective group members together? Separately? Or pick patients from their practices for their group? Would the prospective patients be via referral only? How about the fee arrangements? Meeting time? Group rules if any? Diagnoses to be excluded?

The co-therapist couple then proceeded interviewed eight patients as portrayed by group therapy training class colleagues. They were asked to choose six members for the group. As the series of interviews proceeded the pedagogic drama was interrupted for class discussion, questions, and discussion of concepts. Assessments and informed guesses and hunches were made as to how each prospective patient's own natural life history in groups (family, school, scouts, teams and peer groups), could be used and explored to assess both diagnosis and prognosis for potential effective membership in the therapy group. Some of the students portrayed actual patients they had known in their clinical work. Six patients were chosen for the group.

At the next class session (#2), the students had been asked to think and read about what dilemmas their chosen diagnostic entity might pose in the therapy group to come. The first group session was role-played at class session #3. The group therapy students were quite innovative and accurate in dramatizing typical dilemmas posed by anxiety disorder patients, character/personality disordered, substance abusing and even psychotic members in a therapy group. Stop-action and instant-rely pedagogic techniques were used to discuss and role-play individual group interventions and "group as a whole" process interpretations. Pedagogic role substitution with other members of the class group allowed for lively participation and innovation by all the class group. Detailed discussion of group therapy leadership techniques that might be used by the leaders to handle such prospective dilemmas came to life. No students dozed off as had occurred previous years basic psychopathology lectures.

12

TEACHING STUDENTS ABOUT NARCISSISTIC AND BORDERLINE PATIENTS

Application of pedagogic drama teaching about the clinical treatment of narcissistic and "borderline patients" in groups is intriguing. The use of multiple doubles and rapid role-reversals can demonstrate splitting, projection, projective identification, idealization, grandiosity, sudden devaluation events, and; twin- ship, merger, alter-ego transferences. Therapeutic mirroring and the encouragement of wisdom, humor and the creative process can be accomplished in the pedagogic drama teaching activities of future therapists. Kohut thought wisdom, humor and creativity were higher therapeutic transformations of narcissism. The theoretical work of Kernberg and Kohut, (Object Relations and Self psychology), can come to clinical life via pedagogic approaches. At psychodrama, we can present the narcissistic and or borderline patient with opportunities to resolve his use of splitting, denial, projective identification, and urges for pathological twin- ship, merger, idealization, and devaluation. Standing tall on a chair on the stage during a therapeutic soliloquy or scene with another person can give physical experience to haughty grandiose verbal behavior. Descent of an idealized other person off the idealized-pedestal can come alive as the patient is directed down to sitting on the chair.

Repeated doubling and role-reversals can be helpful with less articulate and less introspective patients... and, those patients with very concrete thinking.

13

PSYCHODRAMA FOR TREATMENT OF NARCISSISTIC, BORDERLINE AND PSYCHOSOMATIC PATIENTS WITH ALEXITHYMIA

In recent decades, psychiatric clinicians have been faced with the challenge of remaining flexible and psychotherapeutically relevant to a broadening scope of patients with narcissistic and borderline personality disorders. Diagnostic sophistication among mental health professionals, increased availability of psychotherapy services, and economic pressures combine to cause the public to expect cost-effective, successful and shorter duration of treatments. These treatment challenges are particularly poignant with the treatment of narcissistic and borderline patients who have meager capacity for insight and limited verbal skills.

Psychoanalysts and psychoanalytic psychotherapists have studied these two diagnostic adjectives in search of full status as nouns. In fact, the very extensive psychoanalytic clinical investigation and theorizing about these Narcissistic and Borderline patients probably played an important part in their inclusion in the diagnostic and statistical manuals (DSMs).

Narcissistic personality disorder and borderline personalities are difficult and complicated to treat even when suitability and positive motivation for psychoanalytic psychotherapy are present.

Some patients with these conditions have the additional misfortune of posing significant difficulty in responding to or making use of verbal based psychoanalytic psychotherapy. If such patients also manifest alexithymia, the task of the psychotherapist is enormous. **Alexithymia,** a term coined by Sifneos in 1972, refers to a cognitive affective disturbance that is characterized by a patient's incapacity to verbalize affect and elaborate fantasy material into words. Alexithymia has been reported in a wide range of medical and psychiatric conditions. When present, alexithymia is an important factor diminishing the success of psychodynamic psychotherapy with patients with narcissistic and borderline personality configurations. Psychodrama techniques add important leverage to the successful psychotherapy of some persons with alexithymia. Psychodrama is an experiential, visual- spatial and action-based large group therapy.

Most inpatient, day hospital or outpatient treatment milieus for narcissistic or borderline patients use large and small group therapy to add a dimension to the psychotherapy approach. The author will emphasize linkages between psychoanalytic theory of treatment and psychodrama treatment theory of narcissistic and borderline patients. The application of psychodynamically based psychodrama can be made to the treatment of narcissistic and borderline disorders. Ego psychology, object relations theory, and self-psychology can be linked with psychodrama theory in the clinical approach to these disorders. Clinical vignettes will be used to illustrate some psychodrama techniques that can be combined with educational, supportive, and group-self cohesion promoting measures for treating borderline and narcissistic patients with alexithymia.

LINKING PSYCHODRAMA AND PSYCHOANALYTIC THEORIES OF THERAPY

I will assume the reader is familiar with the basic literature on object relations theory and self-psychology; particularly the work of Otto Kernberg and HeinzKohut.

The Borderline Patient

> Kernberg in broad terms says psychoanalytic object relations theory represents the psychoanalytic study of the nature and origin of interpersonal relations. The intrapsychic structures deriving from past internalized relations with others is theoretically now re-experienced in the context of present interpersonal relationship situations and conflicts. The therapeutic mobilization and resolution of distorted object relations can be accomplished in psychodynamically informed psychodrama group therapy.

At psychodrama group sessions, pathological internalized object relations and intrapsychic primitive pathological defenses can be enacted and given visual spatial imagery. In a tangible, visual and concrete way the patient can be taught to experience how his or her inner splitting, projective identification, primitive denial and projection operate in the tangible psychodrama setting. Role reversals allow the patient to experience the impact of his splitting and projection on others in his life.

Somatic symptoms can also be represented through doubling and role-reversal techniques. In these situations, a fellow patient or staff member verbally plays the headache, stomachache, or backache. A somatic or psychosomatic state gains concrete, visual spatial psychodramatic reality for the patient to work within the therapy group. The alexithymic borderline patient begins gaining access to his or her inner life through repeated instant replays of family, work or marital situations. Lack of access to the patient's inner life can be lessened through strategic use of multiple doubles representing multiple defense mechanisms or somatic symptoms as portrayed in the psychodrama.

Tangible and repeated use of doubling, role reversal and visual-spatial presentation of and encounter with the patient's real current life behavior, can be balanced simultaneously with psychodramatic parallel scenes exploring related intrapsychic events and pathologic primitive defenses. In fact, such repeated psychodramas for the borderline patient allows for simultaneous portrayal on the stage of inner events, external reality, and even childhood or other past events that influenced his personality development many years ago. Patients can through concrete repetitions begin to put words to these psychodrama experiences. With peer group support and confirmation of the interpersonal validity of these experiences the borderline person can begin to accept and work with feelings that seem inaccessible at purely verbal therapy sessions. The inner world of the patient's splitting, denial and projective identifications become a psychodramatic representational world of the here and now that becomes therapeutically accessible.

We might term these psychodrama experiences "transmuting externalizations" which are not just verbalized but enacted in psychodramatic reality. They become potential sources for transmuting internalizations as Kohut calls such new ego psychological structure building processes in therapy. The patient lives, enacts and sees enacted his splitting, projections and denial. He now could empathize with the results of these intrapsychic proclivities in his relationships. The patient now experiences them in role reversals with his family, work colleagues and significant others on the psychodrama stage.

Let's witness one of many psychodrama sessions with a high level borderline patient and his peers.

THE WAR WITHIN

Pat is a twenty-six- year- old married, Vietnam War veteran who presented to our day hospital treatment setting with the primary complaints of severe headaches and serious family problems. Screening physicians and the neurologist concluded that the headaches were "functional". So far in group and individual therapy sessions. Pat had shown massive denial, projection of difficulties as to his wife or children. His small group therapy members grew resentful and irritated by his reluctance to talk. He had managed to even cause splitting of the day hospital staff who argued about his diagnosis.

<u>The Psychodrama Session</u>

As the usual warm-up phase was being conducted on the day of this patient 's psychodrama, he was sitting quietly in the audience, appearing attentive but tense and with a furrowed brow. The director was proceeding with a loosely structured, bantering-with-the-audience type of warm—up approach. The director gently probed into which life problems had been discussed in any of the small group therapy settings at the day hospital recently. One of Pat's fellow group therapy members suggested that the problem with his headaches be approached on the psychodrama stage because the group's efforts had been ineffectual towards getting him to discuss his "problems".

After a little persuasion, Pat proceeded to the psychodrama stage, where a brief soliloquy and empty chair techniques were used to set the stage for the symptoms of his headaches. They were described as quite intense, pounding, and occurring at least four times a day. The patient often awoke early in the morning with a complaint of headache and would be unable to get back to sleep. Occasionally, he would awake dreaming in the middle of the night with intense headache in the dream. Pat was unable to get back to sleep because of haunting memories of Vietnam. When asked about the most difficult situational dilemma involving his headache, the patient immediately said that arriving home at the end of the day with his family was the most difficult situation.

The psychodrama scene was set for the Pat's coming home where his wife and three children were awaiting. His three-year-old daughter was particularly demanding, clinging, and almost constantly asking him to do things with her and for her as soon as he arrived at the door. His five-year-old son was described as rather passive, serious, and always very supportive towards his father, asking the others not to bother their daddy when he had a headache. This little boy already complained of headaches himself. The three-year-old daughter was incessant in her demands for daddy's attention. The nurse playing her role over-acted the demandingness in the psychodrama scene. Pat laughed out loud.

The first scene of the psychodrama proceeded into the patient's arrival home and a double was assigned to represent the patient's headache itself. The double pounded a chair with a loud, thumping, pulsating sound to accompany his rather harsh comments of torment towards the patient as his psychodramatically represented headache.

Finally, after confronting his family with anger, the patient received superficial support for his retiring to the bedroom to try to ease the headache. After he had left for the bedroom, the family discussed their feelings of being abandoned, not wanted, and pushed aside by daddy. The wife, in a soliloquy, delineated her ambivalent feelings about being supportive towards her husband and her resentment and anger for always having to deal both with the children and with his irritability during the headache episodes. These episodes had become an almost daily occurrence.

While the patient was alone in the bedroom, a fascinating dialogue took place. He was asked to reverse roles with the double who had been assigned to represent his headache. When the patient arrived in the role of his headache, he began to be sneering and tormenting in the tone of his voice. He said, "I got you under my control, baby". The headache spoke of his sadistic joy at restricting the patient's fun, marital, sexual, and family relationships. The headache reminisced about the days in Vietnam when the headaches had first begun. About the long boredom of patrols, and constant anxiety about death, and the responsibility for buddies. Slip-ups in vigilance led to immediate death.

As his own headache, Pat proceeded to describe what he felt were his numerous past sins of getting numerous women pregnant and not caring for the children that resulted. It became very clear as the 'headache" proceeded in his vehement discourse, that in the current situation, the headache acted as conscience for the patient. It did not allow him to "hit the street" to chase women. The headache seemed to curtail any possibility for the patient to go out and dance, drink, or at any time enjoy the companionship of his wife or other social relations. As an aside Pat remarked, "How could I chase other women anyway, I always have the head ache!" Pat's entire superego function seemed to be relegated to the headache. This seemed to come out of an apparent fear of loss of control and the resulting total irresponsibility. When role reversal was completed and the patient once again became himself again, he was asked to express his feelings to this headache that had a spell on him.

Pat proceeded angrily to accuse the headache and curse out the headache for its tyranny of restrictions and guilt provocations.

The director shifted attention to a dialogue between the wife and the "headache" which revealed her great frustrations at her husband's inability to have sex often enough with her because of the domination of the headache. She said, "You are like some strange and enticing mistress, you take Pat away to the bedroom at the very moment that I want him so much." As the "headache" (via a double), was in similar dialogue with his children, the patient learned indirectly about their anger with the headache because of the way it took their daddy away from them and particularly his son's fear that he "might get headaches like daddy when I get older someday".

At the feedback ("share-back") phase of the psychodrama, the patient was struck with the controlling, accusing, and unmercifully conscience ridden meanings that this headache seemed to have for him. He related his intense depression at the early morning awakenings with the headache and noted that they reminded him of the early morning hours of his agonies in Vietnam. He was urged by his fellow group member and by the therapists to take control of his "con science" and personal responsibilities, thus having less need for the headache" to take over these functions for him. Pat admitted that in most group therapy sessions he would have a constant pounding headache, therefore accounting for his silence in group therapy. When asked by the director on the stage whether he had a headache during the psychodrama, he said, "No, at no moment did I have a headache".

At the share-back, other patients in the audience spoke about similar substitute consciences they had via other forms of other somatic symptoms like stomachaches and backaches. Some men spoke about overly dependent relationships with family members, "to do for me." Very supportively, the audience urged him to speak up more in group sessions as he had in the dialogue with his headache.

Subsequent psychodrama sessions with Pat dealt more with his marital and family problems and their connections with his internalized object relations and primitive defenses. A particularly poignant session dealt with his father who had headaches, was a combat veteran from WWII and who had run around with women behind his mother's back. Yet his father had been rigid and inflexible with the patient about his even dating when he was a teenager. Pat confronted his father via a double and auxiliary ego role reversal sequence, where he learned tangible connections between his wish to be a good father and emotional leader in his home and the fear of being a bad, domineering and hypocritical father like his own father.

In one psychodrama session where he and several other patients were reliving combat scenes from Vietnam, Pat did grief work for a benevolent father surrogate he had lost when the older man died at his side in Vietnam. On the same stage, we set up parallel scenes from his childhood home with an absent father, the lost father surrogate in Vietnam and a contemporary scene from his own home. This patient slowly integrated the split off good and bad father images and experienced lessening projection and projective identification onto his wife and children. His family reported that Pat was more comfortable about being an assertive husband and father. Pat seemed to become his genuine - father-himself. Pat became a more verbal small group member at the day hospital. It should be emphasized that psychodrama interdigitated with small group therapy, individual therapy and family treatment.

The Narcissistic Alexithymic Patient

Moreno used the cornerstone concepts of spontaneity and creativity in their interpersonal context. Spontaneous enactment of mental phenomena and interpersonal situations at psychodrama are valued over "just talking about it." These qualities of spontaneity and creativity are combined clinically both to see the same old situation in a new way as well as to see a new and perplexing situation as amenable to some old and familiar wisdom. In no clinical disorder can these cornerstones of psychodrama be more applicable than in the narcissistic personality and its treatment.

The clinical symptom complexes of the narcissistic personality are described as located in 4 spheres:1) <u>the manifest personality</u> (lack of humor, lack of empathy, lack of sense of proportion, tendency to rage reactions, self- deceptive pathological lying to preserve self-esteem and exploitive love relationships always culminating in self-aggrandizement); 2) <u>the social sphere</u> (work inhibitions, delinquent activity of many forms and inability to form and maintain significant, enduring and collaboratively Initiate relationships. 3) <u>the sexual sphere</u> (perverse fantasies and lack of deep sexual interest and intimacy; 4) in <u>the psychosomatic sphere</u> (hypochondriacal preoccupations).

The narcissistic personality is unclear about why he seeks help and the chief complaint is often vague or elusive. These people have highly labile self- esteem and are exceedingly sensitive to slights or perceived slights. At a perceived rejection these patients become bored, vaguely aloof, haughty and depressed, empty or lose zest, initiative at work or become preoccupied with their body, perverse sexual activity, or abuse of drugs or alcohol for self- soothing or acting out of narcisstic rage.

In a 1985 article in the <u>American Journal</u> of <u>Psychotherapy</u>, Goldstein concisely summarizes the transferences of the narcissistic personality.

> "The two extensively described transferences are the mirror transference and the idealizing transference. In the mirror transference, an early need for parental accepting, conforming or mirroring is revived in the treatment situation. In the idealizing, an early need for merging with an idealized parent is analogously revived in the treatment situation. The emergence of these transferences reflects current pathologic narcissistic

> configurations, originating from the earliest times of
> life, secondary to severe absence of various appropriate
> and empathic responses by the parents".7, p.5

This case vignette will illustrate psychodrama combined with <u>relaxation techniques</u> and peer group cohesion promoting use of mirroring, the empathic group as a whole in supportive echoing techniques.

Harold, age 40, is a medically disabled Vietnam veteran who had been at the day hospital for several months. He initially had vague complaints that included headaches and an almost delusional preoccupation with brain tumors. He also felt unable to be happy with his devoted wife and even had constant nostalgic, pleasant but distracting thoughts of affirming Vietnamese girlfriends. He would occasionally brag of his exploits in battle or with women in Vietnam.

The other patients seemed to see him as self- centered but when it suited his need for attention he could act briefly attentive and excessively caring towards others in his small therapy group. The group seemed to strain to accept him as sincere. Harold would act condescending and subtly devaluing to lower ranking staff at the day hospital and lavishly idealizing of the older medical director.

One week he had grown particularly bored with his wife, devaluing of staff, and arrived with more anger and arrogance than usual.

<u>Large Group Relaxation Techniques at the Psychodrama of a Headache</u>; <u>Peer Group as Bio—Feedback Agents</u>
Harold was having one of his daily headaches and sat looking discouraged and tense during the warm-up at our weekly psychodrama. During the unstructured warm-up he finally erupted, "I never have participated at psychodrama here because it seems so silly! But today I just can't stand my headache! I fear I will become violent and tear up this room; I feel like this most of the time.

Harold told of his "workaholism" of earlier years. Now, despite comfortable disability pay, a "beautiful, sweet wife", and all the time he could want to engage in his favorite projects, Harold was incapacitated by daily headaches. He felt that no one at the day hospital or anywhere really cared. He went on and on with his lonely, furrowed-brow discourse about his crippling companion of headache. He seemed impervious to the group members' expression of empathy, gratitude for his help at small group, and some interpretations about his reluctance to accept help or comfort from anyone. He said that these efforts were just as futile as his wife's similar efforts at the breakfast table that very morning.

The director began to set the scene in the kitchen of the patient's home that morning. A fellow patient played his excessively benevolent wife. A parallel scene was set up to one side and behind the present-day breakfast situation. This ghost scene from breakfasts past contained the patients now decreased, ultra-religious, cool controlling and demanding mother and father. These split off introjects were played by two staff members who would comment abruptly, periodically, and with harsh superego attitudes that Harold had discussed at prior small group therapy sessions at the day hospital.

As the action rose in this scene the patient grabbed his head, began to tremble and cry, saying, "I can't stand the pain!" The director froze the action and quickly chose two patients from the small group who Harold trusted the most. They were placed behind and at either side of Harold. The peer patient at the right rear was instructed to place his right hand over Harold's right forehead and his left hand at the right shoulder and neck area. The peer at the left rear was told to place his left hand at the left forehead and his right hand at Harold's left neck and shoulder muscle areas.

The whole audience group was then instructed in progressive muscle tension- relaxation starting from the feet and moving upwards to calves, thighs, abdomen, chest, shoulders, neck, and forehead. The whole group and the patient did these progressively, first on the left, then the right, and then both sides together, Deep breath in and slow breath out was done with each relaxation step. The only two people not participating were the two human biofeedback peer group members. They were instructed to give out a high- pitched sound if they felt tightness or tension and lower softer vocalization if they felt relaxation.

At first, the patient fought the efforts with verbal protests and muscle tensions reflected in piercing peer-produced sounds. As the exercise progressed and the parental presences were moved off stage into the audience group, lower pitched sounds began to predominate. Harold giggled and chuckled at the "share back" phase of the psychodrama. Harold looked and felt more relaxed. Peers from his small group pointed out how subtly controlling and benevolently intrusive he was in much the same fashion as his parents appeared during the psychodrama. Other audience members shared similar experiences "being just like their parents" but not realizing it until group confrontations. Although Harold was skeptical about some of these ideas, he had to admit he felt closer to the group and felt grateful for their help in helping him to relax. In subsequent weeks he seemed to be more open and expressive in his small group therapy. In fact, this type of combined psychodrama, relaxation and "peer contributed bio-feedback" technique seems to enhance group cohesiveness in a striking way.

After this unusual attention at psychodrama, Harold began to accept deeper explorations of his narcissistic defenses at future sessions. Harold's role reversal with his wife with an added double to convey her despair over his entitlement, taking her for granted, and her secret thoughts of leaving him. Finally, Harold began to muster some empathic efforts towards his wife. Harold even laughed at himself at times. He began to reach out to "some of the younger guys" in his group.

At one psychodrama session, he vas barraged with some of his arrogant, devaluing, self-centered behavior as he was requested to role reverse with his wife for the entire session. He finally burst into nervous laughter "Damn! I don't know how she puts up with such a prince."

These modest gains with Harold only came after long hours of empathy and gratifying mirroring and echoing for many months by staff and the group.

"Split—Brain Psychodrama" for an Alexithymic Patient
Bill was a twenty-year-old Vietnam veteran who recently entered the day hospital program complaining of stomachaches and immobilizing depression. In the hour prior to psychodrama, other hospital staff members were conducting an art therapy and educational program. Concepts of the right brain versus left brain functions were presented didactically and were related to some of the patients' art work.

As the psychodrama began, Bill expressed how difficult It was even to draw pictures, much less talk about his feelings in group therapy. In fact, Bill and his wife had had a confrontation the previous weekend when he couldn't even get out to mow the lawn. He wondered why he provoked his wife in such a manner. Once he got out, sweated, pushed and struggled, he felt better; "Even my bellyache got better."

In the psychodrama, the director staged the scene of conflict with his wife. As the scene was set, Bill remarked in passing, "You know, she sounds like my sergeant in Vietnam sometimes". Bill struggled greatly to express himself. A right-brain double and a left- brain double was assigned. As Bill sat in the kitchen with his wife at first pouting and silent, then angry and confrontive, his right brain double of feelings, intuitions, and motivation beleaguered his depressed, immobilized left brain of gloomy cognitions. Bill relaxed as he was asked to reverse roles with his right-brain double and with considerable coaching began to stammer and grow tearful. Bill's headache disappeared and he began to make slow progress in his small group and at marital therapy sessions.

14

PSYCHODRAMA IN THE
HOSPITAL SETTING

In the hospital setting psychodrama can be used on a weekly or twice weekly at a regular time in the unit schedule. This allows patients' small groups and individual therapists or nurses to suggest topics for patients to bring to psychodrama group. Discussion with involved staff after the conclusion of a psychodrama can help with staff education and follow-up of issues occurring at psychodrama in therapy groups and individual therapy sessions.

At unit staff meetings psychodrama can be used to focus on the resolution of staff-patient, staff-staff, staff-physician, or staff family-of -patient problems or conflicts. This use of psychodrama can help reduce staff tensions and facilitate staff education for the sake of patients.

13

USE OF PSYCHODRAMA IN THERAPIST RENEWAL AND BURN-OUT PREVENTION

The playful, active and sublimatory aspects of psychodrama have application for psychotherapist renewal. Freud recommended re-analysis of psychoanalysts every five years. J.L. Moreno talked about creativity in psychodrama as creative when it provides new insight into chronic problem situations and when old wise perspectives can be applied in new ways to behavior. Psychodrama groups offer a vehicle for therapists to share ideas, experiences doing therapy which inevitably involves frustrations, discouragements, and joys related to their personally demanding work. Such therapist renewal psychodramas can assist impaired therapists or just plain tired therapists at retreats with colleagues. They always offer the possibility of new learning and perspectives about psychotherapy work.

Summary:
Psychodrama and its various derivatives and forms can be a remarkably helpful tool in modern psychiatric treatment. It is valuable as a teaching tool called pedagogic drama. Psychodrama can be used as an important adjunct in both outpatient and inpatient settings. For psychotherapists psychodrama can be an exciting, challenging and intensely moving adventure.